CONFRONTING MY
ELEPHANTS

A STORY OF TRIUMPH

RUBI HO

ISBN: 1470060159
ISBN 13: 9781470060152
LCCN: 2012903844
CreateSpace Independent Publishing Platform
North Charleston, South Carolina
Cover art by Alexis Kidd

For...

My brothers and sisters. I love you all very much and would not be who I am today without your presence in my life.

My wife, Yenny, my "honey," my soul mate, and best friend. Thank you for your constant support, sacrifice, and unending encouragement and love. I am truly blessed, indeed.

My son, Christian Samuel, may you envelope yourself with THE Elephant Hunter, live a life without limits, and know you are loved dearly.

Prologue

I was lost for many years of my life. I did not have a sense of direction until my early thirties. Until I found my way, I stumbled more times than I'd like to recount. I've made many mistakes. I've caused a lot of heartache. I created more problems than solutions. I fell victim to the circumstances. Limiting beliefs arose in me.

These limiting beliefs became large. They became dominant. They became like elephants. For a time, they were insurmountable. They controlled me. They forced my choices and decisions. They made me lose direction. They made me question my very self-worth. They pushed me into a state of helplessness. I ran from them as hard as I could. I had no idea where I was going or would end up.

This book is for those of you who might be lost in life like I once was. It is for those without a sense of direction or purpose. You will quickly come to find that I took the cake when it came to being lost. I was the "yes man" of all "yes men." I said yes to every temptation that had to do with money. I hoped that it would help me move forward in life. I only realized afterward that the opposite was true. I ended up more confused and off-track than when I first started.

I want to help people overcome what I call the "elephants" in their lives. Elephants are any limiting beliefs that people have, especially about themselves. They are beliefs that cause people to be less than they really are, less than their greatest true potential. They cause people to be less than their true uninhibited selves. Whether by circumstance, situation, or people, these elephants are created in people's lives, and instead of confronting them, people choose to submit to them.

Here are some examples of "submission":

"I was raised this way."

"Because I never wanted be like my father, mother, etcetera, I made sure I would never…"

"It's in my DNA."

"If I could have only…then I would not be this way."

"If it were not for my…"

"I come from a broken family, so…"

"As a child I heard I would never…so I never…"

"You will never be good enough."

"I wish you were never born."

"I did not get the same benefits as other people, so…"

"If I could live my life again, I would…"

"It's too late and I'm too old to…"

If there is any breath of life left in you, it is time to fight and remove your elephants. Imagine overcoming them, how the release and freedom might feel. If you could live just one day without *any* elephants, any limiting beliefs, just one perfect day, would it be worth it?

Being displaced from Vietnam because of the war, being separated from my sisters, being without a father and a mother, not knowing the English language, living on food stamps, looking and feeling different, getting into fights because kids picked on me, being the only Asian family in a white and middle-class neighborhood, and on and on—there were so many circumstances that I fell victim to and allowed to take over my thoughts and beliefs about myself. Elephants ran rampant and out of control in my life.

Because of my elephants, I became obsessed with not wanting to be different from others. I did not want to be perceived as having less and being less than anyone. I pursued success feverishly but for all the wrong reasons. Looking back, I should have confronted my elephants much sooner than I did. I could have avoided so much unnecessary heartache and suffering. Candidly though, I just didn't know how. Today I know that everything has a purpose, and without my trials I would not be able to share this message.

I will tell you that I am an expert in executive leadership, have master's degrees in organizational management and curriculum design, have written books on coaching, teach people to become executive coaches, and have personally helped hundreds of people to become better leaders. All those things are true, but as my martial arts teacher used to say, "Those things and a dollar will buy me a hamburger at McDonald's."

I believe what ultimately qualifies me to write this book is my personal story, my personal experience, my personal failures, one filled with many moments where I believed I had no hope.

The Departure

*Even though I walk through the valley of the
shadow of death, I will fear no evil; for you are
with me; Your rod and your staff, they comfort me.*
—Psalms 23:4

I was born during the Vietnam War, back in 1971. I was the seventh of ten children. My mom's first husband, Binh, an officer for the South Vietnamese forces, fathered six of them. Early in the war, he was captured by the North and put into a concentration camp. My mom assumed he was dead because that was what happened to many prisoners of war. Being a farm girl with no work experience, my mom's prospects of supporting and taking care of her six kids were practically nil.

At that time, my mom and her children were living in Hue, Vietnam, located in the center of the country, just below the North/South line. Binh's brothers and sisters often came to my mom's aid to help alleviate some of the burden, but my mom knew that situation could not last forever because they were in the same bind as she was. The country was war-torn and in a state of turmoil. There was no stability to be found anywhere.

A few years after Binh's capture, my mom met a Korean businessman, my father. She had four more kids with him: Malaya, Rin, Vi, and me. I am the eldest. I regret that I do not remember my father's name or know who he really was. Being a businessman, he had to travel a lot, often out of Vietnam. During the war's climax, he was in Australia, and due to the complexity and instability of the country, he ended up being stranded there. We would never see him again.

Binh's uncles understood my mom's need to remarry in order to provide for her family. They, too, assumed Binh would never return. But in Vietnamese tradition, it is taboo to marry outside of your race. Since my mom married my Korean father, she was looked down upon by her brothers-in-law. Binh's brothers demanded that they—not my mom—raise her six full-blooded Vietnamese kids. My mom was helpless to defend herself against her brothers-in-law's demands, and so she was forced to give up her kids. Grudgingly and against her will, my mom temporarily let my older brothers and sisters go to live with their uncles. Four of them, Quang, Nhung, Duc, and Bao, went with one uncle, and Na and Van, the two eldest sisters, with the other.

Once my half-brothers and half-sisters were living with their uncles, my mom's "family support" from the uncles ended. So, without any means of taking care of her remaining four children, Mom took us to Saigon, where one of Binh's sisters welcomed her and offered her some help with our care.

Within a matter of months, the whole country was in shambles. The Vietcong was winning the war, and any hope for their defeat was dying. The United States announced that it was abandoning the war effort. Once word spread that the United States was leaving the country, the supporters of the South went into a state of panic.

My mother knew, as everyone knew, that any Southern supporters, civilian or otherwise, were going to suffer extreme consequences from the North, including death. Having been married to an officer of the Southern forces, my mother could not take the chance of being captured. She had to flee the country. She sought help from the only external resource she had at the time: my father.

If there was one life-changing thing my father did for us from afar, it was that he found us space on a small Korean battleship headed from Vietnam to South Korea. But we had no time to spare and were given only a few days to pack up our bags and find our way to the boat.

Since six of her kids were still up north in Hue with her brothers-in-law, she made a desperate plea to them, hoping they would release her children to her. Because of the eminent danger and risks surrounding the trek to Saigon and the hundreds of miles between us and them, she knew the chances were slim that her brothers-in-law would let her kids go, but she had to try.

The uncle who had Quang, Nhung, Duc, and Bao miraculously agreed to my mom's request. The other uncle, who had my two eldest sisters, did not. As Na explained to me years later, he believed that, like the French War, Vietnam as a whole would ultimately be better off and conquer its current trials and troubles despite the civil war. Though he was ultimately correct, this did not happen until many years later.

My mom was able to arrange travel for Quang, Nhung, Duc, and Bao with my oldest cousin, who was only fourteen years old. By hiding in farmhouses at night and taking roads that were not frequented by the Vietcong, my brothers and sisters managed to get to us.

I do not know how it happened, but we made it out in time, all nine of us, one day before the fall of Saigon. With the youngest being only a few months old and the oldest being twelve, my mom, who was only thirty-four years old, managed to get us onto the small battleship. I was four. The only things we had were the clothes on our backs and some bags in our hands. There was no room for anything else.

I can remember moments of that trip vividly. I remember seeing dolphins come up alongside us during the voyage. Without access to any showers and no way to really bathe, daring folks would hang onto a large rope attached to the side of the boat and dip themselves into the ocean. Conversations were infrequent during the entire trip and for good reason: there was not a single soul on that boat who was not leaving someone behind in Vietnam. What was anyone going to talk about? Though we were all grateful for having escaped, the feelings of guilt and desperation from leaving other family members behind to fend for themselves were absolutely disheartening. For my family, it would be two years before we learned that my two eldest sisters were still alive.

One day when I was sitting by myself, a Korean officer popped up from beneath the deck and gestured for me to come his way. More scared than shy, I refused. So he gestured at a young girl who happened to be close to me. More courageous than me, she went down with him below the deck, and a few minutes later she came back with a huge smile on her face and a box of crackers in her hand. I was very jealous.

In what seemed like the blink of an eye, my family made it to Korea and was placed into a refugee camp. We slept on mats in the evening and stayed active within the camp during the day, not really knowing where we would ultimately end up or what was going to happen to us. Besides shelter, there were a few other basic services offered to us, such as daily meals, and there was medical staff on site.

To keep order, meals were served at preset times every day. To avoid a free-for-all, families had to wait to be called up before they could get in line to eat. This also helped families keep track of one another. Regrettably, no one in the camp had birth records, including us. In the midst of the chaos during our departure from Vietnam, there was no time to round up much of anything, let alone birth records. We were who we were, in essence, because our mom could testify as to who we were.

One day, my mom came to us in a panic. She was yelling from the top of her lungs that Malaya, my two-year-old sister, was missing and that she could not find her anywhere. As my sister Nhung recalled the incident, my mom feared the worst: she might have fallen into one of the numerous outhouses that surrounded the camp. We all went scampering around the camp to find her. Suddenly, my sister Nhung screamed out, "There she is!" Believe it or not, she was hungry and had managed to wander off, find a food tray, and put herself into the food line. She had her two-year-old arms up in the air, waiting for the line cooks to put some food onto her plate.

After a month had passed, my mom had to make yet another big decision for our family. An officer from the United States was visiting the camp and was making an announcement to all the families. As the crowds gathered, he started asking—in plain English—if any of us had relatives or connections in the States. Everyone was silent.

Now mind you, there were a couple of things working against this officer. None of us knew the English language. Furthermore, no one trusted him. All of us were downright scared of speaking up. We feared what could happen if we accepted anything this officer offered, considering that the Americans had just "abandoned" the Vietnamese people, including many who were still fighting for their lives, like my sisters. So no one said anything. That is, no one except for my mom. My mom stepped through the crowd and raised her hand high up in the air as if she knew what he was asking.

The truth is we had no family in the United States to speak of. But my mom was not known to hold back. She had come this far, so why stop now? Within a few days, all nine of us were on a plane to one of the largest refugee camps in the States back in the 1970s, Fort Chaffee, which was located in Arkansas. And once again, the waiting game started over for us, but this time on an entirely different continent and in an entirely different land.

Angels on Earth

Blessed are the pure of heart: for they shall see God.
—Matthew 5:8

In the mid 1970s, some American families, particularly those associated with churches, were willing to sponsor Vietnamese refugees to help them get back on their feet again. A few weeks into our time at Fort Chaffee, a family from Denver, Colorado, who were members of a Dutch Reformed church, volunteered to sponsor a Vietnamese family. Their names were Harold and Sib Van Loozenoord, aka our angels on earth. Why we got chosen specifically, I do not know, but I was glad we were.

Harold and Sib already had a family of their own: three daughters, the youngest being seventeen years old. Harold was a printer and a WWII war veteran and Sib was the church secretary. To say the least, they were not born with silver spoons in their mouths, nor were they in a financial state to take on nine refugees whom they did not even know, but they did.

In the summer of 1975, Harold and Sib, along with the help of some friends in their congregation, were able to arrange for us to be flown to Denver, Colorado. Many years later Harold would talk about his first encounter with us at Denver's Stapleton Airport. As he describes it, he and his church friends brought several vehicles to the airport that day because there were nine of us. To their surprise, this was all for naught because we all wanted to stay together and didn't want to go into separate cars. Fortunately someone brought a station wagon, and we all managed to scrunch into that one car.

Before our arrival some of the men from the church made two bunk beds for the boys in my family. When they checked in on us that evening, they found all of us sleeping together on the floor. Our lives were very traumatic back then, and we did not want to be apart from each other for even a second.

As the saying goes, "To the world, you might not be everything, but to one human being, you might be the world." The Van Loozenoords became our world at the time. Harold used his VA loan to buy us a modest home in a middle-class neighborhood known as the Washington Park district. It was here that we started again for the third time. What Harold and Sib did for us qualifies them for nothing short of sainthood in my eyes. I do not think there is anything we can do to repay them for their sacrifice and for making a difference in our lives. They did everything humanly possible and within their control to start us off on the right foot in this country. Outside of the soldiers we had grown accustomed to seeing, they were our first real exposure to Americans. They gave us a home for practically nothing and helped my mom get established with a few cleaning jobs. They gave us a renewed sense of hope. My family is forever indebted to them.

The Beginning

Our inheritance is turned unto strangers, Our houses unto aliens. We are orphans and fatherless; Our mothers are as widows.
—Lamentations 5:2–3

Those first few days in Denver were quiet. We were deep in thought and confused. We wanted some form of normalcy again. In a matter of months, we had fled our home country, left family members behind, and traveled from refugee camp to refugee camp, finally ending up in a place we could not initially make heads or tails out of. We did not know the language. We did not know the culture. We did not know where we were. We did not even know if our sisters were still alive.

What we did know, however, was that we were now living in a foreign land. Slowly but surely we realized that everyone else looked like each other, and we did not look like everyone else. We were the aliens in a foreign country. I did not know what to make of it initially. I do not know how it was for the rest of my family, but I knew that it did not feel good to feel different *and* be so dependent on other people for our well-being. This was the genesis of my first limiting belief in my life, the one that said *you* are different; *you* are less because you do not look like anyone around you.

We were starting completely over again. No one in my family had an advantage over anyone. My mom, as wise as she was, could not help us any more than we could help ourselves, at least in getting acclimated and adjusted to the new life. She was in the same boat. We had no choice and could not look back. As hurtful and as uncertain as it might have seemed, we just had to move forward.

My mom held down two cleaning jobs. That's all the work she could find because of her limited formal education and lack of English. The cleaning jobs were after normal business hours, and oftentimes she would not come home until after midnight.

All the brothers and sisters really missed having our mom around, especially the younger ones. By the time we got home from school, usually my mom had already left for work. Because she got home so late, we were already in bed. The only time we really got to see her consistently was in the early morning, but only for a few minutes since we all had to head out to school. Like clockwork I would get up before the break of dawn and peek out of my bedroom window to confirm that her brown Toyota Corolla was parked out on the curb in front of the house. Once I saw it, I would smile and go back to bed for a few more minutes, knowing that I would be able to spend some time with her later that morning.

As I got older, I would ask if I could accompany my mom to work and help her clean the offices at night. Sometimes she allowed me to come along. It was easy enough for me since all I had to do was empty the small trash cans located in the offices. Once I was done, she would allow me to play around the premises until she was finished. I was as happy as I could be, of course, because I was able to spend more time with her.

Perfectly Perfect, My Mom

A worthy woman who can find? For her price is far above rubies…She rises while it is yet night, and gives food to her household…but a woman that fears God, she shall be praised.
—Proverbs 31:10–30

The dramatic impact of parents in our lives is amazing. We are either trying to emulate them because we grew up admiring them, or we are trying to be the complete opposite of who they are because they were never a part of our lives or were too much over our lives. In the case of my mom and me, I was trying to emulate who she was in her entirety, both the good and bad.

My mom was nothing like June Cleaver from *Leave It to Beaver*. She was a spectacular mom on many fronts, but she was not an absolute angel. She was very street smart and was filled with so much love for people, and she had a lot of drive and a solid work ethic. She was a risk taker and "ask questions later" kind of person.

As closed as the Vietnamese community initially was back in the 1970s, my mom was quite the opposite. Our house had an open door for everyone, including Americans. She would frequently invite people over for barbecues and Vietnamese meals. She never let the language barrier stop her from reaching out to others.

As part of our introduction to the United States, Harold and Sib asked that we attend church with them each Sunday. Though my mom was openly Buddhist, she had no reservations whatsoever about fulfilling Harold and Sib's request. Besides, there was no religious schedule conflict because the Buddhist service was on Saturdays. So every Sunday we would all walk together as a family to the church two blocks away from our house. At the time, there was not one of us in the family who had any real idea what church was really about or why we were really there. It was the least we could do to honor and repay our sponsors.

My mind used to wander off because I could not understand anything the preacher was saying, but one thing kept me coming back enthusiastically every week: punch and cookies. We were a very poor family and did not have those kinds of treats at home. So when I got an opportunity to have the "better things in life," I quickly learned to take advantage of the situation. I would go back as often as I could, or until all the cookies were gone.

In the Vietnamese community, my mom was known as a mover and shaker, a community builder. In fact, in the Vietnamese community my mom became the go-to person if you needed to ship supplies back into Vietnam for family members. We always had tons of boxes in our home because she was responsible for sending supplies back, like clothing and, upon occasion, money.

Back then the Vietcong was known to inspect all packages entering Vietnam, so people had to be clever, especially if they wanted to send back money. My mom had a trick for shipping back money. I watched in amazement every time: she would take a sixteen-pack of Winter Green Spearmint Gum, carefully unwrap it so as not to damage the packaging, and remove the sticks of gum from the foil paper, one by one. She would then carefully fold a twenty-dollar bill into the same shape as the stick of gum and fold the foil right back around it. She did this until she had an entire pack of gum filled with twenty-dollar bills. By the time she was done, you could not even tell the pack of gum had even been touched.

I do not know how my mom managed to take care of all of us, but she did. Part of it is still a mystery to me. Under her protection and ministrations, we always had food on the table and, occasionally, even some special meals, and we always had a roof over our heads. As a mother she was selfless, giving whenever she could. There were times when she would come home late from cleaning and, though she was tired, would exhaust her last bit of energy to be with her kids.

Perfectly Imperfect, My Mom and Me

For by grace you have been saved through faith;
and this is not of your doing but the gift of God.
—Ephesians 2:8–9

My mom had a propensity for stealing. We could afford hardly anything because we were so poor. My mom was terrible with finances and had little education around how to properly handle money. I cannot count the number of times we had to put food back at the grocery store because she did not properly calculate how much it was all going to cost. I was young, but I was still old enough to feel truly embarrassed. I cannot imagine how my mom must have felt, especially with the impatient people watching us, as we had to decide what food to put aside. To avoid future embarrassments, I became very proficient at calculating the cost of our grocery visits and would keep my mom in check once I knew we had reached our spending limit.

Though almost all of our clothes were hand-me-downs, we would occasionally go clothes shopping. I would watch quietly as my mom cleverly changed the price tags on purses or clothes she could not afford to buy. Though I knew in my heart that what she was doing was wrong, I justified her actions by thinking that the store would not miss the price reduction anyway.

When I was eight, there was one time that I manipulated my mom's tendency to steal. We were at the local clothing store, and I had come upon a pair of Donald Duck sandals. When I asked my mom if she could buy me the sandals, she abruptly told me she did not have enough money. This fact did not matter to me, however, and my bratty self started to rant and rave. Giving in, my mom finally told me to remove my shoes as she tore the tags off the Donald Duck sandals. She put my shoes into her purse and had me put on the sandals, and we proceeded to walk right out of the store. Once we were outside, I grinned from my astonishment over what just happened, but I was also thrilled that we got away with it at the same time. I was hooked—with the idea of stealing, that is.

My mom was also into gambling. It was something she had gotten into while she was still back in Vietnam. It was one of her favorite pastimes. She did not gamble in casinos but by playing cards and dice games with her Vietnamese acquaintances in the local communities. Unbeknownst to the public, back then the Vietnamese community would set up mini gambling rooms that were located right in the heart of the ghetto area of Denver. Gambling always happened on Friday and Saturday nights.

In Vietnamese gambling, whether with dice or with cards, people sit in a circle and all the money is typically put into the center as people lay down their bets. I know about such things because many times Mom allowed me to come along. There were at least twenty people in these smoke-filled rooms at every event, and they would play until the early hours of the next day. While my mom was gambling, I would just play with the other Vietnamese kids who happened to come along with their parents as well.

One night at one of these gambling events, the lights suddenly went out. I happened to be right next to my mom at the time. The room went pitch black, and all I could hear were people frantically scurrying and screaming at one another, no doubt trying to protect any money they had. So when the lights finally came back on, it was no surprise to anyone that all the money that had been in the center of the circle was nowhere to be found.

People felt as if they had been robbed in front of their eyes, and in a sense they were. For obvious reasons, no one confessed to taking the money. Tempers flared, accusations and finger-pointing were rampant, and the atmosphere got extremely intense and felt dangerous. One man believed firmly that my mom had taken the pot. I went into panic attack mode as my mom, with the man waving his finger in her face, vehemently denied that she was the culprit. Fortunately one of her friends at the event came to Mom's rescue and was able to push the man back and finally end his harsh accusations of my mom.

"Gambling night" ended quickly that evening. While we were driving home, there was a huge knot in my stomach because of what had just happened. Was there any truth to that man's reaction toward my mom? I just had to know. I looked over at my mom from the passenger seat where I was sitting, and with trepidation and fear in my voice I asked her, "Mom, were you the one who took the money?"

My mom looked me in the eyes as I looked up back at her. Both of our eyes held sincerity and concern. She looked back at the road and, knowing that I was still looking at her and waiting for a response, simply nodded her head.

My mom, of all people, the community leader, the street-smart woman, the one who was so giving to others, was also the one responsible for taking the gambling pot that night.

I was not angered by her actions at all. I did not even feel embarrassed. Instead I was sad, not only for her, but also for my family. It registered to me how much we were struggling to stay afloat. To see my mom go to this extreme really put it in perspective. Will we ever make it out of this mess? Will we ever have a stable life? Will my mom always have to work this hard or go to such extremes like she did this evening? Will we ever be "normal" again?

Looking back, I had no idea of the impact my mom had in my life. I admired her and loved her so much that I associated everything about her with goodness. I could not see wrong in her despite her stealing and gambling vices. She was untouchable in my eyes. She was spectacular with people, admired by many, a friend to all, a go-getter, a risk taker, and a family's provider.

In many ways I ended up becoming almost exactly like my mom because I spent so much time with her. For many years of my life, I almost repeated her same steps—both the good and the bad.

Only now do I realize that we were both trying to achieve the same things and avoid the same limiting beliefs. We were succumbing to the elephant that told us having money was what ultimately would define us and lead us to a better life. It told us that the pursuit of money would ultimately take us from the depths of being poor and show others that we had made it. We believed that having money would ultimately prove to us that we were living the American dream. I believed that having money would lead to wholeness. I started to believe that by having money, I would not feel as if I were less than others.

The Rise of My Elephant

Therefore take up the whole armor of God, that you may be able to withstand all evil that arises in the day, and do all that you can to stand firm.
—Ephesians 6:13

When I was five years old and in kindergarten, Mrs. McCarthy told me one day, "Now, Rubi, tomorrow is your day for Show-and-Tell. Make sure you bring a toy from your home so that you can show it to the other kids and talk about it."

Initially I went into a state of panic. We were too poor to be able to afford toys from the store. My toys were homemade slingshots that I had cobbled together out of coat hangers and used clothes. I also had a broken magnifying glass that I found in my back alley. There was no way I was going to share any of those things. What was I to do?

I was already different, being the only Asian in the class. I did not want to be any more different by not having any toys to share. I didn't even consider asking my mom for money because I knew she did not have any. Besides, she would not be able to buy me a toy anyway, let alone know what Show-and-Tell meant.

So I did what in my mind was the next best thing: I asked Mikey, a boy down the street whom I quickly befriended, if I could borrow his toy Tonka truck for the night. Thankfully he let me. So the very next day during Show-and-Tell, I talked about the toy Tonka truck that I had.

While talking about the truck, there was a feeling of emptiness inside of me because, deep down, I knew it was not mine, and worse, I was lying through my five-year-old mouth by telling everyone else that it was. I had allowed the fear of not wanting to look "poor and less than the rest" take over my morals.

In my view, just saying, "Teacher, I have no toys to share," was practically impossible. The kids probably would have all ridiculed me and laughed, but because I lied that's not what happened. My Show-and-Tell event went off with flying colors. I did such a good job with the presentation that the kids were "oohing and aahing" at my story. Mrs. McCarthy was especially proud of me and let me know about it afterward.

It felt great! I was part of the gang. I was accepted. I belonged. It was at that moment that I decided that I was *never* going to let anyone know how poor, different, or underprivileged I believed I really was. Being accepted squashed all the bad feelings I had initially about lying.

I remember visiting a friend's house after school one spring day when I was in the fourth grade. I was playing outside with my friend Vince, and his father had just come home from work. He parked his car in the driveway, got out of it, and walked up to Vince and myself. Vince said, "Dad, this is my friend Rubi."

With a cold stare, his father looked at me and then at Vince and said, "What are you doing playing with him? Don't you know they eat dog back in their country?" He laughed and then walked away, not giving me another look. When I heard this, it hurt me deeply inside. This man did not even know me. How could he say such a thing and, worse, why? What did I do to him? It made me very angry because it verified that I was different and inferior. Sadly, these kinds of incidents became a very normal part of my life for many years. Incidents like these continued to make my elephant uncontrollable.

To compensate for feeling like I was less, I developed a huge competitive drive and tried to outdo everyone in everything. Not wanting to appear less or have less than others became an obsession. I competed against everyone, from school, to sports, to a simple game of dodgeball. I excelled in school and achieved straight A's for as long as I can remember. I was great at sports, and I picked things up very quickly. When I started something new—anything—I would commit hours and hours to it until I became very proficient at it so I could compete against anyone.

Despite how different I looked on the outside, despite my language barrier, despite my poverty level, and despite my background, I was going to be equal to or even better than the person next to me. It became my drive. It became my addiction. It became how I would avoid my elephant.

They used to call me "Little Big Man" because I always wanted to challenge the older, stronger, and faster kids. During field day events, when kids competed in different races and Olympic-like events, I made sure I had just as many blue ribbons as the top kid in my class. I won district spelling bee championships, was on public television as a kid newscaster for my school, was recruited to go to gifted and talented programs offered by private schools, and, in high school, was all-school vice president. Fitting in and excelling just became a part of my life.

Admittedly the hardest area and audience for me to keep up with and compete against was the financial status of middle-class kids. For the most part, they had parents who could provide all of their basic needs for school and then some. As for the rest of my brothers and sisters and me, we were expected to fend for ourselves. It was not like I did not ask my mom for money. After hearing "no" for so long and seeing for myself what she had to do to obtain things, the expectation of her—or any of my brothers and sisters—being able to help out financially just went out the door. It was up to me to figure out how to make money. At the very least I had to try to keep up with my peers somewhat.

At the age of eight, I started shoveling snow in the winter and raking and mowing lawns in the summer and fall. Since then I have never stopped working. What drove me was not the thought of becoming a millionaire; I just wanted to keep up with what my friends were doing, such as being able to buy candy, T-shirts, or a toy from the store. My motivation was to fit in any way possible.

I would make sure that no one could ever get the idea that I was not "making it" in the States. They could never see me hungry. They could never see me complain. My clothes could never have tears in them. They could never see any weakness or vulnerability in me.

One evening, during a weekly kid's Bible group held at my church, the youth pastor brought out the game *Twister*. According to the rules of *Twister*, a game where people are forced to sprawl out into curious poses onto a color-coded mat, no one is allowed to wear shoes. Inside I panicked because I knew that I had holes in my socks. I was determined that no one would find this out. When my turn came up, I politely declined. Though my friends pushed me hard to play, I did not budge. They finally gave up and left me alone. What they did not know was that I really wanted to play, but the potential embarrassment of having to expose my torn socks to the world weighed heavier on me. I became extremely critical and sensitive of circumstances that shed light on my poverty. Looking back I cannot help but feel a strong sense of shame.

Christmas at my house was a very rare event because we never had any money to buy each other gifts. However, we craved it so much because of what happened our first year in the States. Our church sponsors introduced us to the idea of exchanging gifts by buying each one of us a gift that very first Christmas. It was a very memorable and special event. The fact that we received presents, let alone from non-family members, just blew me away. Naturally, all the kids were expecting gifts the following year, but it just did not work out that way. We quickly realized that Christmas at the Ho house was not going to be a yearly event.

One Christmas morning, a white van with a red shield-like banner pulled up to the curb. I remember yelling to my brothers and sisters when I saw two gentlemen carrying boxes of gifts up to our house.

We were just elated that they had brought us large, wrapped gifts and were truly thankful at the moment that we had received the gifts.

When they left, my older brother Bao was the first one to open his big wrapped box, and my other brothers and sisters eagerly looked on as he ripped open his gift. When he opened the box, we were all silent. From the torn box he lifted out an old, faded magnetic football game. It worked, but it was used. The rest of my brothers and sisters proceeded to open their gifts with trepidation. We were hoping that, at the very least, one of our gifts might be new. But they weren't—not one.

It was not that we were not appreciative of the gifts or that we were angry that the gifts were used. I really believed that, for my entire family, we were all just very sad. Although this was an unexpected visit from the Salvation Army, the fact that the toys were used quickly told me that we had been identified, with very good intentions, as a family that needed help.

I looked at the glass as if it were half-empty. We were identified as a family that had less. I took that very personally. I took it as if I was failing at my goal of showing others that I could keep up and that I was not different. So my obsession with having money grew even stronger.

Deep down inside there was a part of me that knew there was no truth to my limiting belief, my elephant. There was no truth to the idea that, despite my family's poverty level and that we were not like everyone else, we were less. Deep down I knew I was just as valuable as anyone. Every time I would allow myself to embrace this truth, it seemed that yet another situation or circumstance would pop up in my life that would bring out the elephant again. It did not take much. So things got worse, much worse, before they got better.

The Elephant
in Full Form

Be free from the love of money; content with such things as you already have; for God himself has said, I will in no way fail you.
—Hebrews 13:5

One summer morning when I was twelve, a police officer came walking up to our porch and knocked on the door. My eldest sister, Nhung, was the one to answer. I could not understand any of the mumbling. A few minutes later, my older brother, Bao, came into my room. He looked at me and said, "Mommy is dead."

"No way," I replied, pulling back the curtain window to show him her car parked in the street. "See, Bao, her car is right there!"

"She's dead," he said. "That's why the cop is here."

A few moments later, my sister entered our room, tears rolling down her face, and gave us the news. Bao was right. My mom had died early that morning; she was only forty-two years old. She was riding with a drunk driver who ran the car into a utility pole. She died instantly. They were coming back from a night of gambling.

As if the shock of war, being displaced to another country, starting over, not speaking the language, not having a father, and being poor and different were not enough for my family, we were now motherless.

Only one month prior my sister Nhung had turned twenty-one, and she battled to get custody of us. The courts had to make a decision: allow us to be raised by our sister or separate the family and put everyone into different foster homes. I do not know how the judge eventually allowed it to happen, but at the tender age of twenty-one my sister managed to become our legal guardian. We became official wards of the court, which allowed us to continue to receive government food stamps and aid.

I was very angry and frustrated, but I did not want to be. I just did not have any answers to my questions. Why and how could this happen to my family? Why us? Why now? I did not know who to trust or what to believe. I just knew we were going to take two steps backward before we would be able to stand on our own again. My drive to not be poor and different got even worse. Since the sole provider for the family was gone, what were we going to do to keep up now?

My stealing increased. When I did not have money to buy things, I would just steal them—every opportunity I got. I did not let having no money stop me from getting things other kids had. I did not even consider asking my older sister for help. Her hands were already full since she was taking care of us.

One day the following summer, I was on the other side of town visiting one of my friends. I decided to stop at the grocery store in that neighborhood to steal some candy. What I did not know was that it was the worst hit grocery store for shoplifting on that side of town. On my way out of the store, a person standing right at the store's exit stopped me in my tracks and shouted, "What's in your pocket?" He was the store manager.

I was shocked that I had been caught, so I simply spoke the truth and said, "A pack of Starbursts."

He yanked me by my arm, pulled me into his office, sat me on a green chair, wrapped my arms behind my back, and cuffed me. It was one of the most humiliating experiences of my life. I was not scared of the store manager, but I was terrified at what was going to happen when my eldest sister eventually found out.

Until this point I was able to cover up my elephant pretty well. No one in my family knew that I had issues with being poor and different. I kept it to myself. In school, I was a straight A student. So when I got caught shoplifting, I knew there was no hiding anymore.

An officer came and picked me up at the grocery store and hauled me downtown. I had to sit in a confined room until my sister came to pick me up. It was the longest two hours of my life.

When I first saw her, she did not say a word. There was only silence and then, suddenly, a tear rolled down her cheek and she said, "Rubi, I'm very disappointed in you. You are supposed to be one of the brothers that I can depend on and you've let me down. I'm going to have to ground you for one month." That's all she said. I was absolutely devastated.

I would like to tell you that that was the turning point in my life and that I finally broke the chains that bound me to the elephant of being poor and different. That I was "scared straight." But it was not enough. I had not reached rock bottom yet. It was practically impossible for me to stop stealing. I would have had no other avenue to keep up with the Joneses if I did. I had to keep stealing because I was not going to take the chance of becoming fully exposed. That just could not happen. So stealing went on for some time, all the way until I was eighteen years old and a freshman in college.

Alongside my college studies, I was working at a parking booth on the university's campus, giving students parking passes. I was selling half-price parking coupons to students at full price, making about $30 extra every night I worked. One evening, after having been on the job for about three months, my manager suddenly barged into my parking booth and said, "You are done. Get out of here!" I was caught red-handed. A student had reported what I was doing to the front office, and they had been tracking my sales.

After being fired I walked to the bus stop in utter humiliation. I had nowhere to turn and no one to go to. Sharing what happened with anyone would have "blown my cover." That night I went home and wept profusely. I was so ashamed that I never told anyone about it. My sister's words when I got caught stealing candy rang in my mind the whole night. The guilt and shame overwhelmed me. I could not take it any longer.

The very next day, I called my ex-manager. I did not have any words prepared; I just knew I had to call. As the phone was ringing, my heart was beating furiously. He picked up the phone and said hello.

"Mark, this is Rubi." The phone was silent. I went on, "I know you might not believe me at this moment, but I need to tell you that I am sorry from the bottom of my heart. What I did was absolutely wrong, and I am willing to do anything to make it up to you. It was stupid, and I have no excuse." I stopped. There was a pause.

Then he spoke: "You know, I could have had you arrested and sent to jail for this."

"I know, I know," I said, "and that's why I'm calling, just to say I'm sorry and that I'm so thankful you didn't call campus security."

Mark continued, "All I can say is that I'm very disappointed in you. You were one of our best and most reliable workers, and I hope that you turn your life around and stop hurting yourself like this. Good-bye and good luck."

That's the last I ever heard from Mark and that was the last time I ever stole anything. I was extremely fortunate that Mark did not turn me in to the police. If he would have, not only would the façade that I had created been blown away, but worse, I would have been a symbol of shame for my entire family. If my sister Nhung would have found out, she might have never been able to forgive me again. I could not take that chance. That alone ended my bout of stealing—but it did not remove my elephant.

You would think that these kinds of moments in a person's life are enough to turn that person's life around. That is partially true. I did focus much harder on my schoolwork, and I walked a much cleaner, more righteous path. The fear of being seen as less than everyone else still lingered, and my money troubles were far from over.

I still had to make extra money when I could; I just could not resort to stealing. What other way could I make money besides waiting every two weeks for a paycheck that barely covered my bills? That's when I discovered betting on football.

I had friends who knew friends who had bookies. Every week these local bookies would take a minimum of $50 per game. I could afford that, and besides, how hard could it be to cover the spread? During the NFL season, betting on games became a regular weekend thing for me. I could never afford more than $50 at a time, but it did not stop me from regularly betting. The $50 a weekend amount allowed me to justify to myself that it was not really a big deal. Besides, I was not stealing anymore, and it was my money anyway. This rationale went on for the next couple of years.

On the home front, my eldest sister took on the huge responsibility of having to care for me and my brothers and sisters. I cannot imagine the immense burden my sister had to have felt. It was a significant crossroads for all of us.

Duc decided to head off to San Diego with her boyfriend. Quang decided he would stay and help out to the extent that he could. My brother Bao stayed around, too, but he made no commitments.

As for the rest of us, we were expected to help out in whatever way we could, especially around the house.

My sister was very clear that no one could be treated like a dependent anymore. We all had to develop our own independence and act like mature adults as much as possible. No one could take on the role of "mom." They were just as confused and lost as I was.

To survive, we all had to grow up very fast. Ultimately every one of us had to make all of our big life decisions on our own—and live with the ramifications of those decisions. My sister's responsibility was simple: provide us with a home and food on the table. The rest was up to us. She held this responsibility honorably for a number of years, and when my brother Quang got a place of his own, I moved in with him, and he also provided the basic necessities for me.

I stumbled my way through college, transferring three times in three years. I did not know what I wanted to do with my life, but I knew that college would lead to something better, so I did everything I could to stay in the university community. Every year I transferred, the more debt I incurred in student loans and credit cards.

In addition I held down a thirty-hour-a-week job and stayed on the lookout for get-rich-quick schemes every opportunity I got. I also continued gambling on the weekends. In the six years it took to complete my first degree, I had the following jobs: telemarketer, ice cream server, waiter, newspaper deliveryman, remodeler, computer repair guy, janitor, parking booth attendant, and shoe salesman. I also worked in a dinner theater, temporary agencies, and a pizza restaurant. I was never out of work, and except for my parking job, I never got fired. I always ended up quitting because I got bored or I believed I was not making enough money.

There were also many different sales and moneymaking ventures that I sought out. At that point in my life, it did not take much to convince me to try out any scheme for making it big. I used to sell cooking knives and coupon books, got involved in multilevel marketing programs, and eventually got into real estate, the venture that almost destroyed me completely.

At the age of twenty-seven, I married my college sweetheart, best friend, and love of my life, Yenny. She was originally from Venezuela, and I met her at my third college that I attended as an undergraduate. On the surface, my wife saw me as a very intelligent, highly successful, and competitive person doing whatever he could to have a better life. This was the case for my wife as well because she also came from a very poor background. In fact, beginning at age twenty-one, she took on the responsibility of taking care of her father, mother, and two younger brothers. Like me she wanted a better life, especially financially, so as crazy as some of my money venture endeavors were, she supported me, but not without tons of pushback, arguments, and hesitation.

The one thing that she forbade me to keep on doing, however, was gambling. During college she saw how obsessed I had become: I looked over the point spread every week, getting frantic and furious every time I lost, only to come back asking to borrow some of her scholarship money so I could gamble with it the following week.

I would be lying to you if I said it was easy for me to do, but I agreed and stopped cold turkey. To prevent me from being tempted further, I had to completely dissociate from the bookies and my gambling friends. That was probably the hardest part. They had grown so accustomed to me calling them every week that they would go out of their way to have my friends who were still gambling pursue me. Eventually we had to change our phone number and avoid them completely. It was the only way I could stop.

Rock Bottom

He will be with you; he will not leave you or for-sake you. Do not fear or be dismayed.
—Deuteronomy 31:8

I couldn't give up one moneymaking vice without starting up another. Since gambling was officially gone, I had to seek something else to replace it. My fear of being and having less than others was still a huge, rampant part of my life, so I had to find another way to make money. My moneymaking ventures led me into the realm of real estate.

Late at night I started watching real estate infomercials that were filled with people who had nice cars, big houses, and swimming pools. People guaranteed that with little or no money down I could become a millionaire just like them. These people appeared to have stories similar to mine, where they started with practically nothing and ended up with everything. These infomercials easily convinced me that real estate investment could fundamentally change my life. I was hooked yet again. From the age of twenty-seven to thirty-two years old, I went on a real estate tear.

I managed to accumulate over twenty-five pieces of property. I had everything from commercial real estate to single-family homes to apartment buildings. On the surface it looked like I was a real estate mogul. People at work caught wind of what I was doing and often sought my advice on how to purchase and manage real estate. Both were things I had learned to do very well, and I offered them some very sound advice.

My wife and I both had very secure, good-paying jobs. However, because I purchased these properties with little or no money down on my own, I had put my wife and I into severe debt. Almost overnight we were responsible for paying over $15,000 a month in mortgage payments alone. We had over $3.3 million in mortgage debt, and credit cards were piling up.

With nowhere to turn to make ends meet, we kept on applying for more credit cards so we could roll over our debt. We ended up refinancing our home in order to keep up. We were doing everything humanly possible to hold on. Our debts heavily outweighed our income, and we were going downhill very quickly. As the months progressed, I was becoming increasingly desperate and was absolutely dying inside.

This was entirely my fault. I not only put myself into this huge mess, but I pulled my wife into it. "You fool. You idiot," I thought to myself. "Damage and destroy yourself, yes, but your wife too? She is an innocent victim of your insanity." Something had to be done fast. I knew we could not hold on much longer, but with no clear way out in sight, it felt hopeless.

Financially there really was nothing more we could do. Obtaining more properties would just make it worse, and nothing financially drastic was going to happen any time soon. Bankruptcy crossed my mind, and I even brought it up to my wife, but all she had to do was say no to the idea once and I let it go.

Sadly, I was convinced that those properties meant stature. Essentially, my real estate had become that Tonka truck that I showed off to my kindergarten classmates back when I was five years old. I became known among my friends, even among my family, as someone who was "making it," but deep down inside I was just as helpless and empty feeling about my self-worth as I was way back when I was in kindergarten. It had to end.

Confronting My Elephant

For I am persuaded, that neither death, nor life, nor angels, nor principalities, nor things present, nor things to come, nor powers, nor height, nor depth, nor any other creature, shall be able to separate us from the love of God, which is in Christ Jesus our Lord.
—Romans 8:37–39

For so long I was oblivious. My head was in the sand, and I was convinced that I was ultimately in control of my outcome. There was also a part of me that believed I was not really doing any harm. I justified all of my actions somehow. I never stopped to really think and challenge myself by asking if what I was doing was right or wrong, good or bad, for me or anyone else. I needed outside help.

Seeing my wife bite nervously on her fingernails, month after month, as she had to somehow figure out how to make ends meet, I began to realize the toll my endeavors were taking on her. I saw how much I was hurting her. The madness had to stop, but I just did not know how. Running from my elephant had become like a drug to me, almost like an addiction.

When I was trying to get out of my financial bind, I did not learn from the spiritually mature. I clamped on to any overnight program that offered me a way to get out of debt quickly. Time and time again, however, after my initial investment, the programs either asked me for more money or I realized that it was not all that it claimed to be. Before I knew it, I was in a deeper hole than when I first started. I knew I had to do something drastically different from my current approach, but I did not know what "different" really meant.

Everything I had tried financially was failing. There were hundreds of other ways I could try to break free from our financial burden, but I had no room left for error. One more wrong move, and it would be the end for my wife and me. So l looked in the last place that I ever thought I would look for financial guidance: my church.

Ever since my family and I came to the United States, church had always been a part of my life in one form or another. At the very least I learned who God and Jesus Christ were because I was exposed to them at an early age. Candidly though, my so-called "relationship" to God was very superficial at best. For the most part, I knew how to go through the motions. To say I had a sincere and genuine relationship with God was the farthest thing from the truth.

Since my wife was raised Catholic and I had more of a Protestant upbringing, we decided to compromise when choosing a church. To avoid conflict we decided that we would church hop all over the city. We would not pay attention to title, any religious affiliation, or anything else that had to do with identifying what the church's affiliations were. Every Sunday for about two years, we chose a different church to attend. The only criterion we used to select a home church was that we had to completely agree that it was the right place for both of us. After many interesting and eye-opening visits, we ended up in a church in the heart of downtown Cincinnati.

For me, church was a place to worship God and have fellowship with other Christians, and then I was done for the rest of the week. I got to decide what to do with the remainder of my week. Besides, so much of what I knew to be "God's way" was contradictory to what I believed at the time. When my mom died,

I made a conscientious choice to keep God at arm's length. How could someone who is supposed to be all loving allow what happened to our family?

I remember looking up into the night sky a few days after my mom's death with tears running down my face and saying, "God, if you are real, how could you do this to our family? How could you take our mom away?" I did not edge God completely out of my life, but he sure was not going to control most of it. I believed for so long that I could not depend on him, so I spent most of my life putting "control" into my own hands. But being on the verge of financial ruin, I had nowhere else to turn.

The Crown Financial Ministries course being offered at the church seemed like a very non-threatening, six-week, $40 course. The risk seemed low; I had nothing to lose, so I signed up. Pastor Russell Smith was the instructor for the course. Every week I was exposed to what the Bible said about money and finances. My homework was to memorize scripture learned during the week and to complete the workbook that accompanied the class.

During meeting times individuals would share where they were with money and what their struggles were, and then we openly prayed for one another out loud. I was beginning to get something I had not had for as long as I could remember: hope and comfort. The class brought my wife and me so much comfort and hope, mainly because there were people in the group with similar situations—maybe not as extreme as ours, but they realized, as we did, that there must be a better way to deal with finances than what the world said about it.

The focus of the coursework was the polar opposite of what I had been exposed to, and it was refreshing. The theme was direct and to the point: it is all God's at the end of the day. And with God, I was either exalting him or exalting me. The challenge was simple: did I believe this to be true?

The evidence in the scripture was just too compelling and abundant for me to put up a fight and turn away from this and go back to my old ways. So with the 80 percent of my soul that was willing, my wife and I started taking financial steps that reflected "God's way." That was over seven years ago.

Parable:

A rich man came to Jesus and asked what the secrets were to eternal life. And Jesus said, in essence, "You must love your neighbor and live righteously."

And the rich man said, "I do all of these things. Is there anything else?"

And then Jesus said, "Yes, one last thing. You must sell off everything you have, go give it to the poor, and come follow me."

And at this, the rich man's heart dropped. He was saddened and disappointed that Jesus was asking him to give up the one thing that he had built his whole life around. And it was the one thing that the rich man was not willing to do. So he went away.

I played the role of rich man for so much of my life. Just like that rich man, I had allowed my obsession with accumulation to define me. I held onto it as if it was the most important thing to me for so much of my life. Because of my elephant, I was just so afraid to let it go. Little did I realize that by letting go and letting God I was beginning to confront my elephant for the first time in my life.

To be clear, it took us over four years to really get our financial life back on track—four years of very hard work, commitment, and trust. When it did not seem like there was any hope, we just held fast to the faith that we had and kept on the path set before us, until eventually we were able to see the rewards of remaining faithful.

As I write this book today, my wife and I are down to one single property, the one that we live in. Within a few short years, we will finally be free of all our debts, except for our home. We did it not by filing for bankruptcy or through foreclosure. We did it by focusing on God's way. Furthermore and more importantly, I was beginning to learn a fundamental truth: with God in my life, nothing was impossible to overcome, even my elephant.

You might be thinking, that's a good story, Rubi, but what happened to your elephant? What about that limiting belief that overtook your life and said that if you did not have all those things and all that money to define you that you would be worthless? What happened to that?

A person cannot give God part of his life, experience overwhelming success in it, and expect the whole rest of his life not to be affected similarly as well. God does not work that way. What happened to me was no exception.

I naturally thirsted for more. My financial experience with God awakened me to other areas in my life where I might have been excluding God in the decision-making process. I went from being a Sunday-only Christian to having a complete God makeover. I made a conscientious choice to give God the rest of my life.

Once I started to fully focus on a God-centered life, the elephant that used to define me ceased to have any real power over me. In the past everything I did to avoid being seen as having less (such as buying real estate) only made matters worse and made my elephant more powerful. But because God's way around life's problems is not a running and avoiding way but a confronting way, I was forced to meet my limits head on. The more I did that the more the elephant's power in my life dwindled and the more the power of God increased.

Once the noise in my finances got quieter, the next natural step for me was to look at the other big chunk in my life that still had some noise around it, some uncertainty. That was around my career.

Now I want to be very clear in saying, I'm not here to *preach* God onto anyone. In fact, as long as you are not hurting anyone, including yourself, and trying to be *wholly* helpful, you can do whatever you want in your life. I'm just sharing what happened to me, and my story, and my perspective.

Finding Purpose

*Now there are a variety of gifts, but the same Spirit;
and there are a variety of services, but the same
Lord;… To each is given the manifestation of the
Spirit for the common good.*
—1st Corinthians 12:4–7

I believe the old adage "God works in mysterious ways" means that God works in subtle ways, which ultimately means that God works in the silence—the silence of your heart, of your soul, at your center. To be in tune with God within us, we need to become very quiet. In the past I was seeking all of the answers to my questions in the wrong places: places that were not quiet but full of noise, that were full of distraction and temptation.

In the past, my answers and solutions were coming from places that fed my desire to accumulate, to have more—places that fed my desire to avoid my elephant. The more I was avoiding, the more I was accumulating, and the noisier it got around me. I was surrounded by noise, and I became distracted and lost. I realized that all the noise in my life was caused by me running away from my elephant.

Considering what I had been through in my life up to this point and looking at the dramatic effect that God's way had on my finances, I wanted more. More of the "good stuff." More of the "quiet." More of the peace that was starting to fill up my life. And honestly, there was definitely doubt in my heart and my mind that I was in the right place when it came to my work.

So I took another step in my faith journey, but this time pertaining to my career. I was not completely dissatisfied in my career. In fact, I was very successful at what I was doing and getting paid very well for it, but I felt something was amiss. I posed a simple challenge to a profound question: was I living out the life that God intended for me?

In the Bible, Paul challenges us to live out our talents in our life. If you are meant to teach, teach; or if you are meant to be a homemaker, be a homemaker. It does not matter what you do as long as you are living out your special makeup. The Bible teaches us to become our very *highest self* because doing so allows us to fully connect with God and serve others in the way God meant for us to serve.

The challenge for me was to determine what that "one" thing was. What was that one thing I believed I was better at than anyone else? To some people those kinds of questions might sound cocky, but they are not. They are full of truth.

We are all made in the image of our Creator, and as such we come from the greatest of greats. As such we have that greatness in us. If you sell yourself short, that is your choice. Let me be very clear: it is not God's choice that you do not become great. I took on the challenge for myself. Where did I believe I could be great? More importantly, what talents did I possess that could be used to sincerely serve others?

I retraced my life as far back as I could remember. So starting from the age of four and a half, I simply thought about my life, all of it, including my trials, successes, failures, and the people in my life. The critical component in this reflection was to firmly believe the following: although I did not make God a conscientious part of my life in my earlier years, he was always still around. Therein lies the beauty of it all: whether I was a firm believer or not in him, he has always been there whether I wanted him to be or not. Of course I cannot prove this to you, but since reflecting on my life, I believe it.

There have been just too many circumstances dating all the way back from when my family first fled Vietnam, when there was no hope and no rhyme or reason for success. Yet somehow it all worked out. I can only tell you from my perspective that I believe God is always present and just around the corner. Despite how far away you might believe you are from him, he is not ever as far away as you might think or choose to believe.

When I put it all together, I realized that I was meant, in some way, to help the lost. To help people who were not sure of themselves, who were not sure in their direction. To help people who believe they might be out of control. To help people who might even believe they can no longer be helped anymore. To help those who need to become sure of themselves again. Why? Simply put, all those scenarios were part of my life at some point.

Looking back, I realize that all my stumbles in life were not wasted. My trials have been preparing me for my true calling all along. My personal experience in overcoming my lifetime of losses and vices would help me to help others overcome theirs.

I firmly believe that if there is one thing I do and have done naturally for all of my life, it has been to see gaps in things and connect them to solutions. My entire life I've simply been filling in gaps where I saw deficiencies. Because I was focused on the wrong things, it got the best of me. I had put myself into situations where the gaps, especially financially, were endless. Until I chose to have God in my life, I had a leaky bucket that could never be filled.

With my wife's blessing and unending love and support, I started to take firm steps in my career with the hopes of eventually settling in a role where I believed I could more directly help the lost, the people who needed help with direction. Similar to my financial journey, I knew it was going to take some time.

Today, I am president of Rubi Ho Corporation, a strategic leadership firm that helps companies, organizations, and individuals throughout the country become top-level leaders, not through rank or title but by becoming champions in the realm of leadership, character, and positive relationships. I have never been more complete in my life. I continue to author books on executive leadership and coaching and plan to continue writing in areas where I believe I can help others grow and, more importantly, help others become just a little less lost.

Parable:

There was a sword smith who was teaching his apprentice how to properly make a perfect sword—a sword that, once completed, could withstand the most brutal of clashes and could last a lifetime, if not centuries. For days on end, the apprentice's task was simple: just observe. What he saw was how the sword smith would submerge a steel rod into a blazing furnace, remove it after it was in a moldable state, lay it onto an anvil, and beat it into shape with a hammer. Then he would repeat the process. After many days the sword started to take shape. The more the sword took shape, the less the sword smith had to beat it with the hammer and the more he finessed, sharpened, and shined. Finally the apprentice asked the sword smith, "How do you know when you are finished?"

"It's simple," the sword smith said. "I can see my reflection."

In essence, that is how God works in our life. He is our sword smith. It is not that he subjects you to constant beatings. We do it to ourselves. But because of how far off center so many of our choices are, it takes what seems like a beating, for us to get back on the right track. I attribute the turnaround in my life to one simple fact: I started living out a God-centered life. My life did not clear up, become complete and fulfilled until I let go of my vices and turned it over to him. But in the beginning of this process, it hurt, a lot, as if God was beating me up. The fact is, I had many "wrongs" in my focus that I had to make "right." And the more off-focus I was, the more I felt the beating. But as I was starting to take on a renewed shape, which meant a renewed Godly focus, the less it started to hurt. And the more I started to heal and become centered.

The Elephant Hunter

Therefore I tell you, do not be anxious about your life, what you will eat or what you will drink, nor about your body, what you will put on...But seek first the kingdom of God and his righteousness, and all these things will be added to you.
—Matthew 6:25–33

It is not your elephants that I want you to focus on. It is God. Focusing on God naturally takes care of your elephants, but you must know where to start. Almost like an offering, you will be personally giving up your elephant to God and asking for his help in your life.

My elephant was the limiting belief that told me I was different and less than others because I was poor. I allowed it to overcome my life, especially financially. My personal request to God was twofold: I asked him to help me let go of my limiting belief and to help me where I was hurting in my life because of my limiting belief.

For you, it simply starts by going to a very quiet place, settling your emotions and thoughts, and asking yourself where in your life are you truly hurting. Where do you still feel less than complete? Where are you not happy with yourself? And what have been the negative byproducts in your life because of this incompleteness? Elephants cause this incompleteness, and it is these elephants that you must offer up to God so that he can overcome them for you. He is your ultimate elephant hunter. If you are still struggling, see if you might fit into any of the limiting beliefs I presented to you earlier in the book.

Once you have offered up your elephant to God, the next step is to start seeking God's way in your life. That starts by identifying the biggest symptom that arose because of your limiting belief. For me, my finances were a disaster. For others, it could be in their relationships. What is it for you? Where are you hurting most in your life? What in your life must be better? This is where you start seeking out what God says about this area. This is how God starts to become the center of all that you do.

Living out a God-centered life does not mean you have to give up the things in life that truly fill your cup. It only means that you have to let go of those things that have been taking away from who you were meant to become. You have to let go of those things that have made you less than who you really are. You have to release those things that do not have God's guidance in them.

God, above all things, wants your uniqueness to shine and flourish. This is the nature of the creator, but it cannot happen unless you allow him to work in your life. Simply stated, either God is at the center of what you do or you are. One leads to fulfillment, the other leads to incompletion. God wants you to be complete, not empty.

Living out a God-centered life simply means seeking out what God says about the important things in your life and then committing to live out your life through his guidance. By doing so you instantly start to confront your elephants.

I believe that the Bible is one of the best places someone can start to find out what God says about things, but it does not end there. Eventually you will progress from knowing God as he is presented in books and know the real God because of your deep and personal connection with him.

It is okay to be skeptical and have doubts. When you examine the life of Jesus, it is interesting to note that most people did not start believing on pure faith alone. In fact, most of his disciples had what I call an attitude of wanting to believe. It was not until after Jesus performed miracles that people started to turn their attitude into actual belief. Such was the case with the blind man who was made to see again. Only after he gained sight did he go share his story. The same case was true for the paralytic leper begging outside the synagogue. Only after Jesus told him to get up did he start sharing his personal encounter with Jesus. Even Jesus' first disciples did not believe until their nets were overflowing with fish. Why should you be different?

My Encounter

Be still and know that I am God; I will be exalted
among the nations, I will be exalted in the earth.
—Psalm 46:10

One early winter morning in 2011, I was just starting to wake from my deep sleep. The partners from my leadership company and I were spending the weekend at a lodge about an hour away from the city. We were there for our annual leadership retreat. I remember glancing over at my alarm clock to check the time. It was 5:30 a.m., so I still had a few hours before our meeting at 8 a.m. For some reason, I decided I would pray a little differently that morning. Typically I pray out loud, and it does not last for more than thirty seconds, a minute at most. Since I had time on my hands and I could no longer sleep, I decided to try to pray for as long as I could. Mind you, I really had no idea what I was doing.

Having heard a few different meditation CDs from various people I respected, I decided to give "silent" prayer a try. I decided that I would simply say the Lord's Prayer in my mind, but I had one ground rule: nothing could be in my mind before I started the prayer. In other words, my mind had to be empty of everything. I was going to do this for as long as it took to accomplish a quiet mind. Besides, I had two and a half hours, so why not?

Starting out, my eyes were completely closed, my legs were stretched out, I was sitting up against a set of pillows, and my hands were intertwined and on top of my legs. Initially I could sense everything; I wanted to move my hands, scratch my face, think about the day, and notice the vibrating noise of the heat fan. I noticed everything. As thoughts entered my mind, I simply thought to myself, "Let go." I just kept silently repeating these words every time a single thought entered my head. It was a little frustrating at first, but I kept pressing.

Before I knew it, I started to shift my focus to my breathing. At first it felt very intense and sounded very loud, but eventually my breathing got very quiet and started to slow down. Suddenly I noticed that I could no longer feel my hands and my legs. It was as if I knew they were part of me, but I could not feel a real connection to them. They were just there. I could sense that I was becoming more and more aware of the present moment and nothing else. It was exciting.

My thoughts were starting to disappear completely. Strangely, even though my eyes were closed, I started to be able to see again, but differently. It was as if my eyes were wide open but staring directly into my eyelids. I remember just enjoying this newfound experience for a bit—for how long exactly, I cannot say.

It was at this time that I started to say the Lord's Prayer in my mind. Curiously, the only thing that I could say out of the prayer, though, was the word "Father." Nothing else came out of my mind except that word, "Father."

Not wanting to fight or push the moment, I simply said that word and nothing else. After saying the word a few times, the pauses between them started to drastically increase. It was within one of these pauses that an indescribable feeling suddenly overcame me.

Rubi Ho

Instantly I felt absolute comfort. There was nothing inside of me but an indescribable peace—a peace that was void of worry, void of anxiety, void of questions, void of everything but a feeling of completeness.

At that moment, I heard in my very core the utterance "I am" and nothing else. In that utterance there seemed to be an instant understanding of what "I am" meant. To be clear, I did not hear an audible voice. The utterance came from the connection I was experiencing. Nothing else mattered at that moment. I just desired to remain in the state I was in.

After a while, I knew my connection had to end. As I opened up my eyes, I began to cry uncontrollably. I could not stop myself. It was not from sadness; it was from pure joy. It was as if the very essence of me was pouring out and saying, "Yes! God really does exist! I know now for sure!" I was in a state of bliss. Not wanting to forget this moment, I quickly grabbed my iPad and typed out what I believed God was communicating to me. Below is what I typed out verbatim:

Prayer is not about resolving, it's about connecting with God; it's about listening. Resolving before connecting with God is about your will, not about God's will for you

My two-year-old son understands this better than anyone in my family. Before he presents anything to me, he first gets my attention by calling me, daddy, daddy, daddy…he'll do it ten times if he has to. But what he won't do is present or share what he has to share until he knows he has my attention. And for him, he has learned that he achieves connection with me when I

70

physically turn, look at him, and say, yes, son. Then and only then does he share.

As adults we have lost this art. We actually speak before anyone is listening. I don't know if we really care anymore if anyone is listening or if we really want anyone to listen to what we have to say anyway. Why? I believe it's because we don't want to let go of control: control of our lives, our thoughts, our opinions, our goals, our direction.

Unfortunately we can never connect with God that way. We will always be in the way. We must first embrace this truth if we are ever going to connect with God. And that truth is that God is, first and foremost, seeking and longing for connection with you beyond anything else. Actually everything else is secondary. Not, not important, but secondary.

The first place in your life where you must change direction is in prayer. You must focus on connecting first and resolving and requesting second. Realize, I know this is a mind-blowing concept. For some this direction will be achieved the first time around; for others, it's going to take a lot of work. Either way, it must become second nature to you, automatic.

I have a new, simple, first prayer for you, and that is this: Father…

That's it. Repeat it as many times as necessary. Pause as many times as necessary. But each and every time after you say it, listen. Eventually you will hear him. You will feel him. You will be one with him.

When you hear him, then, and only then, do you speak. You share what's in your heart and listen, connect.

71

To be clear, I do not claim to be special. As one of my closest friends, Pastor Russell Smith, often says during his sermons to the congregation, "I am chief of all sinners." I am no better than any other person. I offer no magic bullet. I do know that God is *very* real and *very* personal. He desires a connection with you more than you know or have any idea of. It is with him that you will ultimately find peace. There are many quick fixes out there, but true elimination of your limiting beliefs is found from only one source and that is from your Creator. I believe this to be true. My challenge is that you discover this truth for yourself as well. The place you can begin is through prayer.

Surround Yourself with Elephant Hunters

You will recognize them by their fruits…So, every healthy tree bears good fruit, but the diseased tree bears bad fruit…
—Matthew 7:16–18

Surrounding yourself with elephant hunters simply means associating yourself with God-centered individuals during the times you need both guidance and support. In fact, God never expects you to be alone. There was a reason Jesus sent out his disciples in twos. He knows that we are not capable of doing it all alone and that there are times when we are just not at our very best. He knows that there is no human being on earth who is good at absolutely everything, hence the importance of having a network of support or someone of like mind, intention, and purpose as you.

In terms of "elephant hunting," simply associate yourself with people who are openly making every intention to live out a God-centered life. Mind you, they *aren't* perfect. They don't have to be. When you come across individuals who are truly mature in spirit, meaning their focus is directed towards service and selflessness, their advice comes from a different place. Their focus is different. In short, these individuals are truly centered. There is no ulterior motive and there is no selfishness.

One of the best ways to know whether people are God-centered or self-centered is to look at their fruit. What do they stand for? What are the people surrounding them like? Who do they give the credit to? What are they really trying to accomplish at the end of the day? What is their life's purpose? What are their end-all be-all goals? Do their fruits of success reflect this? Is what they say consistent with what they do?

I'm not telling you to judge them; rather, just look for evidence that proves they are Christ-centered. This world is full of people with great messages and advice, but that does not mean they are Christ-centered. I have fallen victim to these wolves in sheep's clothing many times.

Be okay knowing that there will *not* be an over-abundance of elephant hunters. The fact is we live in a society defined by man and not by God. It is a society geared to tempt you, confuse you, and create an unending desire in you to want more and more of all the unfulfilling things in life. The truth is you will have a lot easier time finding elephants than you will in finding elephant hunters. This doesn't mean you should succumb to the pressures, though, and give up. Elephant hunters are out there; you just have to look.

The good news is that you don't need many. Just a few people who are willing to help guide you and hold you accountable for living a Christ-centered life is all you will need to start veering in the right direction. Remember, God will do most of the heavy lifting once you get set on the right path. I knew I first needed elephant hunters in the financial realm. My search happened to bring me to my pastor and the Crown Financial Ministries course that was being offered at my church. Identify where you need help and where elephants are imposing limiting beliefs in you. Begin finding those elephant hunters who will help you overcome those limiting beliefs.

A Life of Service

But whoever would be great among you must become your servant,…For even the Son of Man came not to be served, but to serve.
—Mark 10:43–45

Parable:

One day at the synagogue, Jesus was standing off in a corner with his disciples, watching as people were giving out their public offerings in the temple. One by one, people would boast out loud how much they were tithing and giving back. Someone would say, I gave 10 percent of what I made this week! Another would say, I gave 20 percent, and yet another, 30 percent! All the boasting occurred so others could hear about how godly they were being in their tithes. As they were boasting to one another, a little woman dressed in raggedy clothes and holding a little cloth bag made her way quietly to the offering alter. Without one word, she opened up her little bag and took out the only two coins she had and gave them up for the offering. It was only at this time that Jesus spoke to his disciples. "Every person who gave will receive their blessing indeed, but no one is greater than that woman, for though they gave from their abundance, she gave from what she depended upon to live. Many times over will be her reward, here and in heaven."

I love this parable. Though it revolves around tithing and money, I think it says so much more about how we are to serve. For one, do not fall into the trap of having to compare your service to someone else's. Leave that to God, because like the boasters in the parable, it is too easy to believe you are either better than or less than another because of your contribution compared to theirs.

It is all too easy to fall away from God's center, even from the point of serving. There are endless examples of people who stand on top of mountains, exclaiming how much they have done in the name of God. I'm going to tell you that God does not want this. Scripture says, "Do not boast about what you've done for me; rather, do it in secret, for I know and see all things and will bless you accordingly."

Why try to serve without boasting? Because God knows how easily we strive to outdo one another and take any chance we get to be ahead of someone else. Even the disciples fell victim to the "totem pole" syndrome. Around the campfire the disciples asked Jesus which one of them was going to get the "higher/closer" seat to him in heaven. Jesus said, "Those who want to be greatest in heaven must first learn to become the least; for I did not come to earth to be a king, but to serve. You must also do the same." Such is the challenge for us when serving. We must be careful not to compare what we do to what everyone else is doing. You have only one true judge and that is God above and no one else. Your "two coins" of service are more than you will ever need to honor God.

Your challenge, through prayer and reflection, is to determine what your "two coins" of service are in your life. Using what talents you have, where can you serve that might make the biggest difference from God's viewpoint?

When it comes to giving back to God, especially around service, some are meant to become influencers and servers of many and some are supposed to only serve possibly one individual.

Though you might want to conquer the entire world with your newfound passion to serve, it might not be how you were meant to serve, at least initially. The key is what Jesus meant when he said that if you would like to serve and follow him but still have troubles with your brother, go first and resolve the issues with your brother. If you still have debts owed to your debtor, go first and resolve your debts to your debtor. Man cannot serve two masters; he can only serve God or money, not both.

You must first make right everything that is not right in your life before God can unleash you fully to serve. God knows full well how hard it is to serve with any type of burden that might be weighing you down. First pursue what is still not God-centered in your life and make that straight. The quantity and quality of your service will go up as your quality of life with God grows. Let that be your first area of service, your "two coins." Allow him to expand your territory of service. Trust that he will.

I'd like to end this chapter with an acronym for you, that when put together, spells out the word: F.O.R.E.G.I.V.E.

I focus on the word "Forgive," because I believe that everlasting peace only comes to those who have learned how to *wholly* and completely forgive.

I call the "Forgive" acronym, the Forgiveness Principles:

F stands for "face your fears!"

O stands for "Own your life!"

R stands for "Revel in resolution!"

G stands for "Give of yourself!"

I stands for "Include inspirational things and people!"

V stands for "Value yourself as much as God values you!"

E stands for "Embrace the fact that you are limitless and eternal!"

The Challenge

I still stumble every day, if not in my actions, then in my thoughts and intent. But I hold on to one very simple, yet profound truth: I was made in God's image. Knowing this gives me completeness. Knowing this gives me wholeness. Knowing this gives me peace. Elephants no longer run my life. I no longer run my life. God does.

I would like to conclude this book by having you read the following statement of truth:

With God's breath, you were created to be great, you were created to be limitless, and you were created to be free. You are to use your greatness, that greatness that God breathed into you, to ultimately serve others. There is no greater purpose than this.

My prayer is that you embrace these truths, and live a limitless, God-centered life. Seek out God in everything you do. It is he who will give you peace, comfort you, guide you and fill your cup. It is he who will confront your elephant. God will be waiting, patiently and lovingly. You need only ask.

Here's your challenge: Become an elephant hunter for someone. Make an open commitment to them, encourage them, support them, and help them confront any elephants they might have in their life. Simply plant the seed and let them make the choice. Share my story. Share yours. And allow God to do the rest.

Let the elephant hunting begin...

—Rubi

About the Author

Rubi Ho is a well-regarded strategic and organizational consultant, celebrated author, and founder and architect of the Strategic & Organizational Consultant (SaOL™) methodology and consultant certification program.

With an extensive background in organizational management, curriculum design, strategic leadership and executive coaching; Rubi has devoted his career to pioneering methodologies that transform the way organizations communicate, collaborate, and lead.

Logging over 30,000 consulting hours "in the trenches" with companies and their leaders, Mr. Ho's direct and candid approach to consulting and issue resolution has earned him the trusted respect of CEO's and their teams. Versatile and scalable, he has worked with over forty companies transcending industry and company size including Procter & Gamble, Marathon Petroleum, Speedway, MISO Energy, United Way, Peach State Freightliner and ORR Corporation.

Through this work, Rubi recognized that organizations are naturally unhealthy creating the inspiration for *Many Parts, One Body.* Energized, he origi-nated the Strategic and Organizational Leadership (SaOL) methodology, an integrative framework to identify – and resolve – organizational "pain points."

Now a proven leadership platform, Rubi has created a national certification program educating other re-nowned Business Consultants in the ways of SaOL.

These **SaOL Certified Consultants** today are help-ing countless organizations strategically drive com-petitive advantage through organizational health and performance.

Visit www.TheRubiHoGroup.com to learn more about SaOL and how SaOL Consultants can make organizations and its leaders healthier.

(513) 489-4900

info@therubihogroup.com

Other Books by Rubi Ho

Many Parts, One Body

Healthier Leaders, Healthier Teams, A Healthier YOU

Made in the USA
San Bernardino, CA
14 August 2016